EARTH'S ENERGY RESOURCES

NATURAL GAS ENERGY

ELSIE OLSON

Consulting Editor, Diane Craig, M.A./Reading Specialist

Sandcastle

An Imprint of Abdo Publishing
abdopublishing.com

abdopublishing.com

Published by Abdo Publishing, a division of ABDO, PO Box 398166, Minneapolis, Minnesota 55439.

Printed in the United States of America, North Mankato, Minnesota

052018
092018

THIS BOOK CONTAINS RECYCLED MATERIALS

Design and Production: Mighty Media, Inc.
Editor: Liz Salzmann
Cover Photographs: Shutterstock
Interior Photographs: iStockphoto, Shutterstock, Wikimedia Commons

Library of Congress Control Number: 2017961701

Publisher's Cataloging-in-Publication Data
Name: Olson, Elsie, author.
Title: Natural gas energy / by Elsie Olson.
Description: Minneapolis, Minnesota : Abdo Publishing, 2019. | Series: Earth's energy resources
Identifiers: ISBN 9781532115547 (lib.bdg.) | ISBN 9781532156267 (ebook)
Subjects: LCSH: Natural gas as fuel--Juvenile literature. | Power resources--Juvenile literature. | Natural gas--Prospecting--Juvenile literature. | Energy harvesting--Juvenile literature. | Energy development--Juvenile literature.
Classification: DDC 553.285--dc23

SandCastle™ Level: Fluent

SandCastle™ books are created by a team of professional educators, reading specialists, and content developers around five essential components—phonemic awareness, phonics, vocabulary, text comprehension, and fluency—to assist young readers as they develop reading skills and strategies and increase their general knowledge. All books are written, reviewed, and leveled for guided reading, early reading intervention, and Accelerated Reader™ programs for use in shared, guided, and independent reading and writing activities to support a balanced approach to literacy instruction. The SandCastle™ series has four levels that correspond to early literacy development. The levels are provided to help teachers and parents select appropriate books for young readers.

EMERGING • BEGINNING • TRANSITIONAL • FLUENT

CONTENTS

ALL ABOUT NATURAL GAS ENERGY

We use energy each day!

It comes from many sources. Natural gas is one source. It is a fossil fuel.

Natural gas formed from dead plants and animals in **swamps**.

Heat and **pressure** turned their remains to gas. This took millions of years.

Natural gas is found in rock.

It fills tiny holes called pores.

Most natural gas is deep underground. People drill wells.

The gas flows up the wells. It goes through pipes.

Natural gas can also be made from coal. This was called town gas.

Town gas lit lamps in the 1700s.

Robert Bunsen was a **chemist** in the 1800s. He invented the Bunsen burner. It uses natural gas.

Scientists use Bunsen burners in experiments.

Today, pipes bring gas to homes.

People use the gas for heat and cooking.

Power plants burn natural gas to make electricity.

Natural gas pollutes less than oil or coal. It also costs less.

But drilling for natural gas can harm the **environment**.

Scientists are working to fix this problem.

THINK ABOUT IT

Have you used natural gas energy? What did you use it for?

GLOSSARY

chemist – a scientist who studies what substances are made of and how they change.

environment – nature and everything in it, such as the land, sea, and air.

fossil fuel – a fuel formed from the remains of plants or animals. Coal, oil, and natural gas are fossil fuels.

pressure – the force of something pressing against something else.

source – where something comes from or begins.

swamp – an area of wet land often partly covered with water.